20

Life Lessons

FOR YOUR
FORTIES

Farima Wassel Joya

7reasures
PRESS

Printed in the United States

20 Life Lesson Series, Vol 3
20 Life Lessons for Your Forties

First Edition

By: Farima Wassel Joya

ISBN-13: 978-0-9986611-2-4 (7 Treasures Press)
ISBN-10: 0-9986611-2-0

Library of Congress Control Number: 2018907086

Published by 7 Treasures Press
www.7treasures.com
7tpress@7treasures.com
(510) 275-3497

To my loving sisters:

Ferozan
Nargis
Homaira
Avista
Mari

Introduction

Life is an interesting journey. As time passes by, you grow up without noticing anything different from day to day. You have the opportunity to become mature after passing through every obstacle that comes your way. Each obstacle teaches you a unique lesson that only you can experience. For the rest of your life, you will follow your knowledge and wisdom to go through your life journey as an individual. From time to time, you will realize that what you have is not enough, and that is when the need for reading and learning from other people's experiences comes in handy. People share their wisdom in the hope of making a difference in other people's lives. The 20 Life Lessons for Your Forties are humble yet unconventional lessons that will help you make your life a pleasant journey.

If the average age expectancy of our times is eighty years old, you are at the beginning of the second phase of your life. It is as though life is giving you a second chance to start over. This is the time to evaluate your life and reinvent yourself a life that you always wanted to have. At this point in life, most people are dealing with older kids and teenagers in their families. Life is as demanding and hectic as ever. Every member of the family has their own schedule, agenda, and desires. Your forties might be your last chance to enjoy the company of your children and your family life. Take advantage of it and do your best to teach your children by example how they should be when they are on their own in a few years.

By many accounts, philosophers looked at a person's forties as being a turning point. It is a time to reflect on what you have accomplished and if you are living the real life that you wanted. Most of you will have regrets about things you did not do, or the route that you did not choose. Soon, once your children are off to college, you'll have a chance to reset. Some call this time in life the midlife crisis, but in reality, this is a chance to start over. However, keep in mind that abrupt or unexpected changes in your life can affect your children, spouse, and everything that you have built so far in a very negative way. If you want any changes to happen, make sure to do it with your loved ones' advance knowledge.

Life is short, and it looks like about half of it is already done. If you haven't had a health scare, you might have one soon. If you have not had a loss in your life, you should expect it by now. This is the time to grow spiritually and improve your physical and mental health for the benefit of yourself and your loved ones.

You might be very happy with your life, but time moves on and you will need to change with time as well. I hope these 20 Life Lessons will help you move forward towards your life's journey and serve as a guide toward your inner desires and living a purposeful life. I only wish that you utilize these lessons and find your own path in life with ease and joy.

Sharing Is Caring

I share these 20 life lessons with my five sisters, all of whom are about to begin or have just begun their forties. I love them, count on them, and will do anything in my power to be there for them. As a family, we always take pride in being the best daughters, best wives, best mothers, and best individuals we can be. I am blessed to have each one of them in my life.

I write this guide with the hope that you will share it with your loved ones. Wisdom is always a great gift that can brighten someone's life with just one word or phrase. After reading it, please pass it on to someone you love and care for a lot.

Farima Wassel Joya

"Life begins at forty."

W.B Pitkin

20 Life Lessons for Your 20s

Just in case you did not pick up a copy of 20 Life Lessons for Your Twenties, here is your chance. Some people are further along, and some are behind with their age-related activities and maturity, but you can start from today and from wherever you are in life now. It's never too late to do the right thing. The lessons are listed below.

1. Forget planning for the rest of your life

2. Make a vision board

3. Give your parents a reason to trust you

4. Detach from your old friends & make new ones

5. Develop a unique character trait

6. Take your finances seriously

7. Pick your role models but follow your heart

8. Be active

9. Plan a solo trip

10. Explore art

11. Don't get emotionally involved

12. Monitor your community, country, & the world

13. Avoid self-destructive behaviors

14. Admit you don't know

15. Say no to peer/parent pressure

16. Speak your mind

17. Trust your guts and take risks

18. Help people to help you

19. Find your passion

20. Be flexible and adaptable

Keep these lessons in mind and practice them if you are not already doing so. Now, are you ready for the most valuable life lessons for your thirties?

20 Life Lessons for Your 30s

It will also help you to know the 20 Life Lessons for Your Thirties.

1. Live your unique way

2. Forget your childhood

3. Your family is your priority

4. Have a hobby and a sanctuary

5. Have a financial plan

6. Buy your first home

7. Change careers

8. Volunteer

9. Go on vacations

10. Spend time with family and friends

11. Have an open mind

12. Find ways for venting your frustration

13. Form a new relationship with your parents

14. Eat healthy

15. Learn to meditate

16. Exercise

17. Clean your clutter

18. Be present in the moment

19. Stay positive

20. Be curious

1

HAVE FUN WITH FAMILY

You are likely to be busy with your career and work most of the time, and most likely you have a spouse and children you love and care for very much. You are always in a rush and short for time. And, as you know, time flies and you will not be able to turn back the clock. You need to make good memories for the members of your family. You will need to spend more time doing fun family activities because you might not have the chance to do so in the future. The kids are growing older every year and their needs and wants change. As they move from being kids to preteens, teens, and adults, they build their character and personality. They each are very unique and if you don't try to know them now, it might be too late. You can go on camping trips, go fishing, play sports activities at the park, go shopping, bake, cook, clean, and organize together. Your time with your family is the most valuable asset that cannot be replaced by anything. When the time is gone, it's gone forever.

Sometimes, you procrastinate and postpone your fun and leisure time with your family without realizing how fast time moves on you. You will miss the times to know them and recognize their uniqueness. Be part of their growing up if you would like them to have a friendly relationship with you when they are adults. Making good memories for them is an essential part of your job as a parent.

2

Fatima Wassef Joya

Support Individual Creativity

It is up to you to support and shape your children's individuality and bring out their unique character. They all have something special about them that everyone should know, and that uniqueness should be strengthened. Great things can be achieved by using a person's strengths. Make sure they recognize their strengths as well, and use them as much as possible.

If your kids are into sports, drama, music, art, science, nature or any other subject that interests them, make sure you have additional resources available to them. If they show interest in any extracurricular activities, make sure they can take part in them.

When we realize our children's behavior or character is shy, reserved or introverted, or on the other end of the spectrum, intimidating, social and extroverted, we need to know how to teach them to deal with their own unique personalities in school or any social setting.

Now is the best opportunity for you to shape your child's future and support their creativity in a positive and safe setting without criticizing, judging or pushing them to be something that they are not.

Positive rewards are the best way to bring out the best in them.

3

Recharge Yourself

Recharge yourself physically, mentally and spiritually. Because you have so many responsibilities and so much work to do at home and outside of the home, you deserve to take short re-charging vacations regularly. You can go for a one- or two-night mini-vacation in your town or the next town closest to you. You can make it a date night with your spouse, or time away with friends if you want to be with other people. The point is to go somewhere new and do something new.

Make a special occasion for a concert that you attend, or just a night out of town. Visiting nature is always inspiring and relaxing. Find the closest hiking trail or the secret hideaway spot in your town. Try to choose somewhere that puts you in the most relaxed mode possible. A place that makes you forget your daily chores and routine—a place to inspire you to stay motivated.

Taking these short trips not only rejuvenates you, but it'll give the rest of your family the space and time to do what they want to do. It becomes a breather for everyone to have a fresh start.

If you haven't started practicing meditation yet, now is the time. The purpose of meditation is to quiet your mind. Before you get comfortable with sitting still for a period of time, try to start the process by taking a day off and spend it all by yourself doing nothing; walk in the nature all by yourself; indulge into a fun activity, or just rest and breathe as if there's no problem in the world.

4

INVEST IN PASSIVE INCOME

Now that you have a steady income and a good job, it might be a good time to discuss finances with your family. You need to be a good role model for saving money, as well as making money. Your choices now are a very important influence on how your kids feel and think about finances. Not having enough money is not a reason to have a negative attitude towards money. This dilemma will always be present. No matter how much money you earn, there will be people who make more than you. So, if you try to chase money, you'll end up losing precious time that you take away from your own health and the relationships that matter most to you.

At any budget and income level, there is always a chance to invest in something that can make passive income for you. You need to take this opportunity and have your money work for you. These are some of the possibilities for investments that create passive income:

- Write a book or an ebook and sell it online
- Have a blog on a subject that interests you, build a community, and run advertisings with Google AdSense
- Become a silent partner with another business through crowdfunding sites
- Create a local business where you can have other people work for you and still make a profit
- Sell your own products online
- Buy and sell real estate by yourself or in a pool with other investors
- Rent your unused space
- Collect referral fees
- Build an app
- Create an online course

5

READ BIOGRAPHIES & NON-FICTIONS

This is a time in your life to learn things that you always wanted to but never had a chance to learn before. Learn more about spirituality, finances, leadership, relationships, and everything else to arm you with wisdom.

Believe that your knowledge and experience has brought you so far, and if you want to go somewhere that is beyond your imagination now, learn about it. There's almost nothing in our world that has not been explored, so instead of inventing a new wheel, you'll need to build upon the existing knowledge. Or, look at knowledge from a different angle and use it to improve the quality of your own life.

How-to books are a great way to learn things that you did not know before and want to try to experience. If you've never cooked before, try a few good recipe books; if you were ever curious about your health, invest in some good health-related books. With computers and tablets, information is always at our fingertips. Although information is not always enough—you'll need to put your new knowledge into practice and take some action.

Reading inspirational and motivational people's biographies can be a priceless motivation. We'll learn firsthand how and why a person reaches a high level of achievement in any area. Perhaps when reading biographies, we can think of our own lives and how they unfold. Is your life story worth of writing, and one that will inspire others?

6

PUT YOURSELF FIRST

You are almost closing the door to your midlife; you are halfway done. Now, you must ask yourself if you have the body and energy to go for another forty years. Just like any other time in your life, regular exercise and healthy food is critical right now. Some people might be too busy to pay attention to their own health, but if your health is declining, your whole life will decline.

By 40, our body feels tired, and we are emotionally asking ourselves if we are on the right path of life. Sometimes, this is the time that major changes happen: kids grow up, divorces take place, we lose parents or friends, our careers are demanding … all of these can be very stressful. One way to reduce stress and keep on going is by being physically active. You need your body and health to go a long way without any sign of fatigue for you.

Your body needs regular exercise more than at any other time in the past. Make sure you do something that will become a daily routine habit for you. Make exercise the most important part of your lifestyle.

Please remember that there is no tomorrow. You will be a day older tomorrow, and your body will not be the same even if you are still breathing. Time does not stop or put you on hold at a particular age or shape. You'll grow older and weaker day by day, whether you believe it or not. Exercise, healthy food, and plenty of rest keeps you younger and healthier.

7

DEVELOP YOUR HOBBY

If you don't have a hobby, get one, and if you have a hobby, develop it further to become a part of your lifestyle.

You will eventually have some free time down the road and the best thing to fill up your time is to be busy with your hobbies. Life is very unpredictable, and you never know if there will be a time that your life and livelihood will depend on how busy you are with something that you love.

When you are busy doing something that you love, your body is aligned with your emotions and makes you feel good. Research has shown that hobbies or leisure activities boost the immune system and creativity, reduce stress, give you a good night sleep, and improve flexibility and memory.

Your hobby can be something that you want to do for free because you enjoy doing it. However, you are free to change hobbies whenever you'd like to. When you think you are done or want to experiment with something else, that is the time to add another hobby and develop it further to challenge yourself to new levels of accomplishment.

Sometimes it happens that the time and money that you have invested into your hobby will pay off as a financial reward. The things that you have collected or learned to build or have created become valuable. Your knowledge on your hobby becomes valuable as you can teach others how to do it. Always think of your hobby as an investment for a future business adventure or something that you can give back to the community by sharing your knowledge.

8

Roshan Wessel Jones

BE OK WITH IMPERFECTIONS

These are the beginning stages and you will soon realize that life is not perfect, and it will remain imperfect. Not only it is okay to live an imperfect life, but it's okay to celebrate the imperfections of your life. Often, things don't work out the way you want them to work out; it will make you upset and you become frustrated for a little while. But, this is the reality of life.

Emotionally, we create an image of a perfect set, perfect life, perfect conversation, perfect partner, perfect children, and perfect community in our mind. These are images we see in magazines, in movies and on our television sets. But reality is not a movie or a picture in a magazine. Life is ever-changing and dynamic and cannot stand still at one point or position. What we have today might not be ours tomorrow, and what we don't have today, we might get tomorrow. We plan, and act on our plans, and think we have the control ... but unfortunately, we don't have control of many things in our lives. So far, most of our decisions, actions and behaviors have depended on other people and situations. But, if we don't already, very soon we will realize that expecting an imperfect life might be the perfect way to look forward to life from now on.

In fact, our abilities and skills in dealing with the imperfections of life give us the fuel, the motivation and the energy to tackle one task after another.

9

KEEP YOUR INTEGRITY

In our forties, we are mature enough to know that difficulties are part of any normal life. If anything proves to be valuable for the remainder of your life, it is that you keep your integrity and values all the time. This is the primary trait of people who can be trustworthy leaders and role models for your children and the younger generations in your family.

Coming to a boil, getting frustrated easily, having anger, losing your temper, and raising your voice or crawling under the blankets in a dark room are not good characteristics to grow old with. If we want to live by example, this is a time to look at the difficulties in the face and go through them with integrity.

At this point, we might have already seen death, destruction, war, hunger, and hopelessness in our lives. Every one of these situations is a reminder that the good and the bad go through cycles and one comes after another. Neither will last forever, but what will last forever is your integrity. It's okay to cry, to make mistakes, to fail, to admit your mistakes, to apologize, and to suffer losses, but it is not okay to stay down, lose hope or sell yourself short. There's light after the dark, and the best solution is to remain optimistic in any situation that we are in.

10

PEOPLE'S PERCEPTION IS WRONG

You are at an age that you might have given value to what other people think of you in the past. By now, you might have already realized that people's perceptions about you are wrong. Everybody makes their own judgement based on their own information in their mind, which has nothing to do with you. In your twenties and thirties, it's very important to feel you fit in, to make friends and to feel part of the normal crowd, but in your forties this need becomes less and less important. You will realize that you only need a small number of supportive friends and your family members to hang out with. In your forties, you realize that your wishes, dreams, and goals are more important than what anyone thinks about you. In your forties, not only do you realize that everyone's perceptions about you are wrong, but you start to not care about it.

You are a unique person with unique values, talents, and capabilities. Many people, including people very close to you, might not know everything about you, and they will never know—and that's okay. You will move on to live and be your true self every day and let people make any judgements they want. In the end, it's your life that matters.

At the same time, you should never compare yourself with others for the same reason. Your judgement might not be right about the other person either. You are only responsible for your own actions, your own decisions, and your own life. If you make a mistake, own it and move on; if you accomplished one thing, move on to the next thing, thinking that there's only one of you in this universe and that is you with no comparison. You'll do your best at everything you do, and you'll live life based on your own standards, not anybody else's.

11

LEARN TO SAY NO

This is the age to stand up for yourself and be comfortable saying no without hurting any feelings. At this age, your priorities shift from your family and career responsibilities back to yourself. This is a critical time to mind your physical and emotional health, and not to push yourself harder to tolerate more than you are capable of. At younger ages, you can drink more, you can stay up late at night, you can hike for twelve hours, and you can work twenty-four hours, but now you'll need a very good reason and plenty of recovery time if you do any of these activities. Eventually, you'll have to say no to some of these activities and to some close friends. It's better to learn to run your own agenda than to be in an unwanted situation.

You also might be guilty of pleasing everyone in your life so far. Now might be the time to put a stop to that by listening to your own body and emotions to say no in a very polite way. You will start living life on your own terms, and that means that you need yourself with your full attention to do that and take some unwanted or undesired activities, people, or situations out of your life.

By opting not to participate in an unwanted activity, you are freeing up time physically and emotionally to work on your hobbies, your health, and your personal development, or to spend it in whatever way brings you more joy.

12

By now, you have a good understanding of reading your instincts. During your twenties and thirties, you were trying to fit in and look normal or like everyone else. However, your forties are the time to find yourself and what you stand for. What are your values? Are they the same as the common beliefs, or do you have different ideas? Make your values and points of view known and understood by your family and community.

There are many things that you don't agree with and it is obvious that you can't change many of them, but for the ones that you are in control of, you need to stand up and speak up about it. Change them to your way.

In order for you to make a difference, the world needs to hear you out and bring your desires and ideas to life. If you are not clear about your ideas and using your instincts, try to focus your thoughts through meditation. Through meditation, you'll gain access to your true inner desires and you'll have a solid understanding of what you want and what you stand for.

At the community level, make sure your voice is understood about your political views, your kids' school policies, systems and procedures at work, and even dealing with your friends and family during community events and special occasions. You'll build your character as a leader who cares to improve things rather than someone who does not care much and follows the rules. Don't be afraid to make your own rules if the current rules do not work or do not make sense for you.

13

MAKE YOUR BUCKET LIST

Life is too short to postpone doing the things you love to do. Up until now, you were busy with building your family and career, but now is the time to fulfill your desires and dreams one by one.

People never regret things that they have experienced, but you will regret the things that you always wanted to do and never did because of one reason or another. This is the time to pat yourself on the back and acknowledge that, whether you feel successful or not, you have accomplished something. At least you lived for forty years, day in and day out. Now is the time to list every wish that you have. You might not be able to make them a reality now, but this activity will put your mind in the right direction for accomplishing everything that is on that list. The purpose is to map everything you want to do before it's too late.

Luckily, not everyone wants the same things, but when you put your desires on paper you get one step closer to knowing them and to fulfilling them. You will find support, resources and people who are interested in similar activities, and your dreams will become a reality sooner than later.

Making your bucket list and your vision board is something that works for you subconsciously so that when the opportunity arises, you'll know how and when to grab it.

14

COMMUNICATE CLEARLY

In your forties, you don't want miscommunications to disappoint you. You are dealing with teenage children or young adults and your spouse of a few years. Usually people get used to each other and assume that they know each other. Sometimes, your kids surprise you with things that they know and can do that you were never aware of or did not believe were possible. For this reason, it is very important to give clear instructions and set your expectations according to your instructions.

When you expect based on your assumptions and expectations, you set yourself up for failure and disappointments. Almost all family disappointments happen because of miscommunication or not communicating at all. You receive the greatest joy in your life from your family, and so it is with your greatest disappointments. And almost every time, you try to blame others for not understanding you correctly. But, does the fault lie on other people not understanding you, or is it you not communicating clearly? The only way out of family drama is to never assume anyone will perform according to your wishes within yourself.

Only if you put in the efforts for clear instructions, honesty, transparency, and sincerity to communicate will you receive the same back.

15

KEEP ROMANCE ALIVE

Although each spouse is busy with his or her roles, duties and responsibilities, they still have a need for their emotional belonging, touching, caressing and intimacy. This is perhaps the crucial age when most physical changes occur: weight gain, baldness, some wrinkles. These changes are very subtle and show up one after another, which is a normal part of aging. Both partners might have fantasy desires for someone who their spouse is not in the shape of their twenties and thirties. However, intimacy and sex is not only a physical attraction and need; it is also a spiritual connection and an emotional need as well. The partners might not have the same physical attraction as before, but the relationship changes more to a sense of belonging and satisfaction.

It's very easy to take each other for granted and get lost in daily activities with family and career issues and lose the sense or the need to look good. However, keep in mind that the desire for sex and intimacy will exist through your eighties and even your nineties. You might be done through the first round of sexual urges, but the purpose of sex after your forties is more emotional than physical.

Clear communication with your spouse about how your personal needs and desires have changed throughout the years is crucial. You've grown older and so has your spouse, but make sure to be open and talk about your desires, wishes, and wants.

Sex is a sacred, joyful activity that has physical, mental, and spiritual benefits when it is about connecting to the heart, body and soul of another person.

Go the extra mile to make each other happy. Surprise each other, buy gifts, indulge and pamper each other, celebrate every special occasion, and take lots of short weekend getaway trips to keep romance alive.

16

Review Your Habits

You already know what your good and bad habits are. Although your bad habits are part of your identity by now and people have gotten used to them and expect them from you, if you are growing up and want to improve yourself for the future, change them.

Some habits are destructive physically, such smoking, drinking excess alcohol, and staying up too late, and some habits are damaging emotionally, such as pretending you're something that you are not, or constant competition with your neighbors or colleagues. Maybe you've never opened your mail, you've never cleaned the bathroom, you've never put your socks away, you've never picked up after yourself. Perhaps you've smoked cigarettes, used alcohol, partied a lot, or never visited a sick person or attended a funeral. Well, now is the time to change. You are now in a position where others are looking up to you, and chances are that you have kids that are learning from you. In that case, always think about what you want your children to learn from you.

As you drop your bad (or out-of-date) habits, you can pick up or add things that you want to see more of in the future. If you admire a habit in a person, maybe that's something that you want to adopt as your own. New, healthy habits build your character and move you towards being the person you always wanted to be. Your good habits will be a source for attracting happiness, health, money, success, and positivity in your life.

17

EXPOSURE TO UNHAPPINESS

Your children are under eighteen and you've been protecting them, providing for them, and keeping them happy all the time, but it's also important for them to understand and go through hardship and feel the necessary pain and suffering. By experiencing these things, they'll be able to make better decisions and feel less pain every time they face a negative, stressful situation. Kids will always look up to the older ones for answers and direction on how to deal with difficulties in life, especially separation, loss, and disappointments.

Let them know you have financial issues, tell them about your dissatisfaction with relationships, and talk about your struggles so they know how to deal with integrity in those situations instead of demanding something that causes extra hardship for you now, and later in their own lives.

There are three ways of dealing with tough times:

1. You'll lose it yourself and you don't care about anyone but yourself. You'll see yourself as a victim and won't hesitate to share your pain and disappointment with your family or close friends every chance you get.
2. You'll run away from pain and difficulty and ignore your feelings and the feelings of everyone around you. You think that by ignoring it, you won't feel the pain. You keep it all inside yourself.
3. You'll acknowledge the pain and difficulty in real time; you evaluate your reality, share your vulnerability with your family, and ask everyone for understanding and patience as you believe in your core that good times and bad times are only temporary.

You don't need to wait for unhappiness and bad times of your own life to expose and teach your children about hardship. Sometimes, kids learn the most valuable lessons of their lives when they visit places and people who are less fortunate than themselves. Visit the homeless shelters and food banks and volunteer regularly; help out through your local churches. Take your kids out of the country to a poor country where they are exposed to how people live with less privileges than are available for them.

18

LOVE & ACCEPT YOUR CHILDREN

You've come so far and have given all your energy and talent, and worked hard to raise your children. You might have had expectations of how your children will do and how they'll be, but very soon you realize that they each have their own individual personalities, habits, dreams, and desires.

You'll question your own parenting sometimes, but you'll need to understand that it is not your job to shape their future. Experience has shown that five kids raised by the same parents, loved equally and well cared for, have different lifestyles and different futures.

As parents, all you can do is to guide them to reach the potential of their dreams and desires. It is not about what you want for them; you'll need to guide them to use their inner strength and talents to build their own future. Your role is to be that supportive parent to offer unconditional love and a space that they feel safe, and trust you enough to fall back on you if they make mistakes.

Never let your child's character, personality, or choices be a cause for your embarrassment. You already know that people will talk down, criticize, or openly object to your children's choices, but your job is to stand behind them instead of forcing your children to be or do something that they can't.

There's nothing worse in the world than the feeling of not having the support of your parents or a trusted person to share the emotional pains of growing up with. Again, you'll need to understand how your child turns out to be has very little to do with your parenting or yourself. Children are born with their own personality, and you'll either let them shine it or suppress it with your actions. Suppressing your child's personality is likely to cause physical, emotional, mental and social suffering.

19

ALL ADULT RELATIONSHIPS

You are closing your midlife stages and if your parents are still living, keep an adult-like relationship with them. Although they may require more of your time and attention later or when they are in need, your relationship should be a reciprocal one. You do to them as they do to you. Set expectations if you or they have special circumstances, but this is the time to enjoy and use each other's company for the mutual benefits of each other. You can't use them, and they can't use or abuse you. Obviously, if you can spoil them and treat them, do it, because they spoiled you and are willing to give up their entire life for you. The payback time begins soon.

Keep the same relationship with your siblings—a reciprocal one. You are not responsible for them and they are not responsible for you, but as a family you always stand up for each other. However, family should count on each other in times of need. Your part is to be there for them, help them sort through their difficulties, and continue their lives.

You'll need to keep in mind that although you want your close family's comfort and happiness, you won't be able to make them live a happy and comfortable life. You'll do your part as much as you can without sacrificing your own personal and family obligations. You always understand who your priorities are in life that depend on you, what are temporary family hardship times, and when your involvement in family matters affects your health and personal relationships. You'll always lose something to gain something else.

When it's necessary to take responsibility for your parents, siblings, nieces, nephews or cousins, that's when they become a part of your immediate family and a priority in your life.

20

FORGIVE EVERYONE

Your life might not be the way you wanted. Unexpected things always happen and it's part of any normal life. If you haven't forgiven people who harmed you in the past that have shaped your life today, now is the time to do it.

Sometimes, it is nobody's fault that we have ended up where we are in our forties, only the result of our own mistakes and wrong decisions. Now is the time to forgive yourself and move on.

Consider your forties as the end of your youth and the beginning of another chapter of life. This is the time to move on to your own way of life and move towards achieving your own desires with joy and peace. The only way to do this is to let go of all grudges and negative thoughts about anyone who held you back in any way—including yourself.

You can start with a clean slate and try to write your own life story from where you are. Only you are responsible for your future and how it turns out.

More than half of your life is remaining. If you want to make it count, make sure you can go to the end on your feet. Keep up with your physical, mental, and spiritual health. Let go of all baggage that you might have been carrying until now and look forward to a new and exciting chapter of your life in your fifties.

About the Author

Born and raised in Afghanistan, Farima lives on the Hawaiian Islands and enjoys a blissful life. She is a happiness life coach, speaker, author, and a practicing yogi on the path to self-discovery and higher spirituality. Rumi, the 13th century Persian scholar, inspires her.

Author of:

- How to Live Your Life with 7 Treasures You Own
- 20 Life Lessons Series

To read her blogs on Happiness Within and find out more information, please visit:

www.FarimaJoya.com
farima@farimajoya.com
Message: 510-275-3497
Facebook: @farimawjoya
Twitter: @farimajoya

Much gratitude to you for going through the 20 Life Lessons for Your Forties.

Now, what to do?

If you want to give back, please leave a short comment to let me know what you found useful in this ebook, and how it can be helpful to your life.

www.farimajoya.com/shop/
20 Life Lessons For Your Forties

Share Your Love 😊